Keto Recipes for Beginners

Quick and Yummy Low-Fat Recipes to Heal Your Body and Lose Weight

Isabelle Lauren

Table of Contents

BREAKFAST

1. Baked Custard - Dairy-Free

Preparation Time: 20 minutes

Cooking Time: 1 hour

Servings: 6

Ingredients:

- Unsweetened - full-fat coconut milk (3 cups/678 g)

- Raw eggs (4 large/200 g)

- Pure vanilla extract (1 tsp./2.5 g) or scrapings from ½ of

  a vanilla pod

- Optional Sprinkle Topping: Nutmeg/cinnamon

Also Needed:

- Glass baking dish - to hold serving containers

- 6 oz. glass custard/serving dishes

Directions:

1. Warm the oven to 350 °Fahrenheit.

2. Boil enough water to come ½ inch from the top of the outside of the custard cups. Place the cups into the pan. (Wait to fill the dish with water.)

3. Whisk the eggs with the milk, sweetener, and vanilla and add it to the cups. Sprinkle cinnamon/nutmeg over the top as desired.

4. Arrange the holding tray on the oven rack and pour the hot water to make the water bath. Bake the custard for 45 minutes.

5. Check for doneness. Insert a knife into the middle of the cup. It's ready if it comes out without custard attached.

6. Carefully transfer the dishes to the countertop or serving tray to serve. Add any leftovers to the fridge with a covering of foil or plastic wrap.

Nutrition: Calories: 246 Net Carbohydrates: 3 g Protein: 6 g Fat Content: 24 g

2. Old-Fashioned Baked Custard

Preparation Time: 20 minutes

Cooking Time: 1 hour

Servings: 6

Ingredients:

- Water (.5 cup)

- 36% heavy cream (2.5 cups/565 g)

- Raw egg (4 large/200 g)

- Pure vanilla extract (1 tsp./2.5 g) or Pod scrapings (½ of

  a vanilla pod)

Optional Toppings:

- Sweetener - your preference

- Nutmeg or cinnamon

Also Needed:

- Glass baking dish

- Glass custard dishes (6 oz.)

Directions:

1. Measure and boil water to make a water bath using the baking dish. It needs to be enough to extend three-quarters of the way up the custard cups (fill in the last step).

2. Set the oven to 350° Fahrenheit.

3. Use a mixing container to whisk the eggs with the water, vanilla, cream, and sweetener - if using.

4. Scoop the custard into the serving cups. (Place the cups in the baking dish before you begin.) Sprinkle using a dusting of the nutmeg or cinnamon to your liking.

5. Arrange the baking dish on the oven rack. Pour the hot water into the ½-inch marker of the cups.

6. Set a timer to bake for 45 minutes. It should be firmly set. Test it using a knife in the middle of the custard. If it comes out mostly clean, it's ready.

7. Serve the custard warm. Store it with a covering of foil or plastic in the refrigerator.

Nutrition: Calories: 370 Net Carbohydrates: 3 g Protein: 6 g Fat Content: 37 g

3. Bacon & Egg Bombs

Preparation Time: 15 minutes

Cooking Time: 30 minutes **Servings: 6**

Ingredients:

- Bacon slices (4.2 oz. Or 4 large)

- Large organic eggs (2)

- Ghee or butter (.25 cup)

- Black pepper (1 pinch)

- Salt (.25 tsp.)

- Mayonnaise (2 tbsp.)

Directions:

1. Set the oven temperature at 375° Fahrenheit.

2. Arrange the bacon slices on a parchment paper-lined baking tin. Bake it; / for 10 to 15 minutes. Drain and reserve the grease.

3. On the stovetop, boil the eggs for ten minutes in salted water. Quickly add them into an ice bath to cool. Peel and slice the eggs and add the butter or ghee to the eggs. Smash with a fork.

4. Combine the pepper, salt, mayonnaise, and bacon grease. Stir thoroughly and place it in the refrigerator for 20-30 minutes.

5. Meanwhile, crumble the strips of bacon in a container for breading the bombs. Form six balls using an ice cream scoop for uniform sizing. Roll them in the bits and place them in the fridge.

Nutrition: Calories: 185 Net Carbohydrates: 0.2 g Protein: 5 g Fat Content: 18 g

4. Scrambled Eggs

Preparation Time: 5 minutes

Cooking Time: 5 minutes

Servings: 6

Ingredients:

- Eggs (4 large)

- Salt and pepper (as desired)

- Skim or 1% milk (.25 cup)

- Fresh parsley (2 tbsp.)

- Cooking oil spray (as needed)

Directions:

1. Finely chop the parsley. Break eggs into a bowl and add the milk, pepper, salt, and parsley. Whisk until thoroughly combined.

2. Warm a skillet using the med-high temperature setting and lightly spritz it using the cooking spray.

3. Pour eggs into the pan, pushing them around the pan with a non-metal spatula until the eggs are set, and no liquid remains (5 min.).

4. Scrape the pan and continue stirring to keep the eggs light.

5. Note: For the best results, don't use egg beaters! They will not properly cook.

Nutrition: Calories: 161.5 Net Carbohydrates: 2.9 g Protein: 13.7 g Fat Content: 10.1 g

5. Cheese Eggs

Preparation Time: 3 minutes

Cooking Time: 4 minutes

Servings: 6

Ingredients:

- Butter (1 tbsp.)

- Eggs (2)

- Soft cream cheese with chives (2 tbsp.)

Directions:

1. Heat a skillet and melt the butter. Whisk the eggs with the cream cheese.

2. Add to the pan and serve when ready.

Nutrition: Calories: 341 Net Carbohydrates: 3 g Protein: 15 g

Fat Content: 29 g

6. Ham & Egg Cups

Preparation Time: 5 minutes

Cooking Time: 20 minutes

Servings: 9

Ingredients:

- Fresh eggs, fresh (5 large/250 grams)

- 36% heavy cream (.5 cup/135 grams)

- Natural Uncured Black Forest Ham by Applegate (7 oz. Pkg.)

- Coconut oil (5 grams/1 tsp.)

- Also Needed: Muffin tin (at least 9-count)

Directions:

1. Set the oven temperature at 425° Fahrenheit. Lightly grease nine wells/cups of a muffin tin with a spritz of cooking oil.

2. Arrange one slice of ham in each of the muffin wells/cups, pressing the ham's slices into the cups centered with the ham covering the sides and bottoms.

3. Whisk and thoroughly combine the cream, egg, pepper, and salt. Fill nine of the muffin cups.

4. Bake until the egg centers have puffed, and the eggs are set (7-10 min). They might slightly jiggle - if shaken but shouldn't be runny/liquid.

5. Add desired garnishes such as green onion or roasted red peppers, or feta cheese, but add the extra carbs.

Nutrition: Calories: 117 Net Carbohydrates: 0.96 g Protein: 7.72 g Fat Content: 9.17 g Calories: 117 Net Carbohydrates: 0.96 g Protein: 7.72 g Fat Content: 9.17 g

LUNCH

7. Cream Cheese Stuffed Peppers

Preparation time: 5 minutes

Cooking Time: 10 minutes

Servings: 4

Ingredients:

- Organic baby peppers – 6

- Cream cheese, full-fat – 6 tablespoons

Directions:

1. Rinse peppers, pat dry with paper towels, then slice the top off.

2. Remove seeds from each pepper, then stuff with cream cheese until full.

3. Serve immediately

Nutrition:

Calories: 145

Fat: 12 g

Protein: 3.7 g

Net Carbs: 6.7 g

Fiber: 1 g;

8. Keto Artichoke Dip

Preparation time: 5 minutes

Cooking Time: 5 minutes

Servings: 20

Ingredients:

- Frozen spinach – 10-ounce

- Artichoke hearts, chopped – 14 ounce

- Cloves of garlic, peeled – 3

- Onion powder – 1 teaspoon

- Mayonnaise, full-fat–½ cup

- Parmesan cheese, grated and full-fat–12 ounces

- Cream cheese, full-fat–8 ounces

- Sour cream, full-fat–½ cup

- Swiss cheese, grated, full-fat–12 ounces

- Chicken broth, organic–½ cup

Directions:

1. Switch on an instant pot, place all the ingredients except for Swiss cheese and parmesan cheese, and stir until mixed. Shut an instant pot with its lid, sealed completely, press the manual button and cook eggs for 4 minutes at high pressure.

2. When done, let the pressure release naturally for 5 minutes, then do quick pressure release and open the instant pot.

3. Add Swiss and parmesan cheese into the instant pot and stir well until cheeses melt and are well combined. Serve immediately.

Nutrition:

Calories: 230.7 Fat: 18.7 g Protein: 12.6 g Net Carbs: 2.6 g

Fiber: 0.7 g;

9. Keto Taco Meat

Preparation time: 5 minutes

Cooking Time: 8 minutes **ervings:** 8

Ingredients:

- Ground turkey – 2-pound Diced white onion–1/2 cup

- Diced red bell pepper–1/2 cup

- Tomato sauce, unsalted–1 cup

- Taco seasoning–1 1 /2 tablespoon

- Fajita seasoning–1 ½ tablespoon

- Avocado oil–1 teaspoon

Directions:

1. Switch on the instant pot, grease pot with oil, press

   the 'sauté/simmer' button, wait until the oil is hot,

and add the ground turkey and cook for 7 to 10 minutes or until nicely browned.

2. Then add remaining ingredients, stir until mixed and press the 'keep warm' button.

3. Shut the instant pot with its lid in the sealed position, press the 'manual' button, press '+/-' to set the cooking time to 8 minutes, and cook at a high-pressure setting pressure builds in the pot. The cooking timer will start.

4. When the instant pot buzzes, press the 'keep warm' button, do a quick pressure release and open the lid.

5. Transfer taco meat to a bowl, top with avocado slices, garnish with cilantro and serve.

Nutritional Info: Calories: 231 Fat: 14 g Protein: 21 g Net Carbs: 2.5 g Fiber: 1.5 g

10.   Green Beans with Bacon

Preparation time: 5 minutes

Cooking Time: 4 minutes

Servings: 4

Ingredients:

- Slices of bacon chopped–5

- Green beans halved–6 cups

- Salt–1 teaspoon

- Ground black pepper–1 teaspoon

- Water–1/4 cup

- Avocado oil–2 tablespoons

Directions:

1. Switch on the instant pot, place all the ingredients in it except for oil, and stir until mixed.

2. Shut the instant pot with its lid in the sealed position, press the 'manual' button, press '+/-' to set the cooking time to 4 minutes, and cook at a high-pressure setting pressure builds in the pot. The cooking timer will start.

3. When the instant pot buzzes, press the 'keep warm' button, do a quick pressure release and open the lid.

4. Transfer the greens and bacon to a dish, drizzle with oil, toss until well coated and serve.

Nutrition:

Calories: 153

Fat: 9.2 g

Protein: 7 g

Net Carbs: 4.4 g

Fiber: 5.6 g

11.   Keto Beef and Broccoli

Preparation time: 5 minutes

Cooking Time: 25 minutes

Servings: 4

Ingredients:

- Chuck roast, sliced–1 ½ pound

- Broccoli florets–12 ounces

- Garlic cloves peeled–4

- Avocado oil–2 tablespoons

- Soy sauce–½ cup Erythritol sweetener–¼ cup

- Xanthan gum–1 tablespoon

Directions:

1. Switch on the instant pot, grease the pot with oil,

   press the 'sauté/simmer' button, wait until the oil is

hot and add the beef slices and garlic and cook for 5 to 10 minutes or until browned.

2. Meanwhile, whisk together sweetener, soy sauce, and broth until combined.

3. Pour sauce over browned beef, toss until well coated, press the 'keep warm' button and shut the instant pot with its lid in the sealed position.

4. Press the 'manual' button, press '+/-' to set the cooking time to 10 minutes and cook at a high-pressure setting; when the pressure builds in the pot, the cooking timer will start.

5. Meanwhile, place broccoli florets in a large heatproof bowl, cover with plastic wrap and microwave for 4 minutes or until tender.

6. When the instant pot buzzes, press the 'keep warm' button, do a quick pressure release and open the lid.

7. Take out ¼ cup of cooking liquid, stir in xanthan gum until combined, then add into the instant pot and stir until mixed.

8. Press the 'sauté/simmer' button and simmer beef and sauce for 5 minutes or until the sauce reaches the desired consistency.

9. Then add broccoli florets, stir until mixed and press the cancel button.

10. Serve broccoli and beef with cauliflower rice.

Nutrition:

Calories: 351.4

Fat: 12.4 g

Protein: 29 g

Net Carbs: 11 g

Fiber: 8 g;

Dinner

12.   Keto Beef & Broccoli

Preparation Time: 10 minutes

Cooking Time: 15 minutes

Servings: 4

Ingredients:

- 1 lb. of beef - ex. sirloin, skirt steak, or flank steak

- 2-3 cloves garlic

- 1-2 heads broccoli - broken into florets (or pre-cut bagged)

- 2 pieces of ginger

- Ghee or olive oil

Optional to Garnish:

- Sesame seeds

- Chopped scallions

The Marinade:

- 1 tbsp. + 2.5 tsp. sesame oil 1 tbsp. Red Boat Fish Sauce

- 4 tbsp. coconut aminos - divided ¼ tsp. - baking soda

- ½ tsp. sea salt 3 minced garlic cloves

- 1 tsp. - ginger

- ½ tsp. of black pepper - divided

Optional: ¼ tsp. crushed red pepper

Directions:

1. Combine the ingredients for the marinade and

   sauce (in two separate bowls) and set aside.

2. The Marinade: Two tablespoons of coconut aminos, ½ teaspoon of salt, one tablespoon of sesame oil, and ¼ teaspoon of baking soda.

3. The Sauce: Mix the stir fry sauce by combining two tablespoons coconut aminos, one tablespoon fish sauce, two teaspoons sesame oil, and pepper.

4. Slice the beef into ¼-inch thin slices and place in a pan with the marinade for at least 15 minutes.

5. Chop the broccoli (or take it out the bag if using pre-cut). Put it in a safe microwave bowl with two tablespoons of water and cover. Microwave for two to three minutes until it is tender but still has a crunch. Place it to the side for now.

6. Warm a skillet or wok using the med-high temperature setting along with one tablespoon olive

oil or ghee. Mince and add the garlic, ginger, and salt. Sauté them for about 15 seconds.

7. Crank the temperature setting to high and add the marinated beef. Be sure to evenly distribute it and cook for around two minutes (without moving it about too much) until the edges are dark – then flip and repeat.

8. Final Step: Add the sauce and stir-fry for about one minute. Mix in the broccoli.

9. Toss it further for another ½ minute and toss to serve.

Note: This recipe calls for coconut aminos, but you may substitute it with a gluten-free soy sauce or Tamari. However, you will need to use half the amount to achieve a more robust, saltier flavor.

Have you ever used Red Boat Fish Sauce before? It is a Vietnamese fish sauce that pro chefs often use to create that elusive "fifth flavor-umami." It is made using black anchovy and sea salt with no added msg or preservatives. Each tablespoon of the sauce has 4 grams of protein, 15 calories, and -0- carbs and sugar. It is gluten-free and keto-friendly. Remember, this is the secret to the recipe: For this Keto Beef and Broccoli to be on point, you need to marinate the slices of beef for at least 15 minutes.

Nutrition:

Calories: 255

Protein: 28.2g

Carbs: 9.2g

Fat: 12.4g

Fiber: 2.4g

13.   Chicken Salad

Preparation Time: 10 minutes

Cooking Time: 30 minutes **Servings:** 4

Ingredients:

- 32 oz. of low-sodium chicken stock

- ½ tsp. salt ½ cup of mayonnaise

- 1 ½ lb. chicken tenders 2 tbsp. - celery – finely minced ½ tsp. ground black pepper

- 2 tsp. dry ranch salad dressing mix

Directions:

1. Poach the chicken in the chicken stock. Use an oversized pot to prepare the chicken stock and chicken tenders. Poach them for 15 minutes. You

can extend by another five minutes to cook or until the chicken is thoroughly done - not pinkish.

2. The next step is to shred the chicken. You can use one of two methods for this. Choose a paddle attachment and shred with the stand mixer. The chicken tenders can also be shredded with two forks.

3. Take a bowl that is of medium-size. To this, add mayonnaise, dry Ranch dressing mix, celery, black pepper, and salt. Stir these well, and combine thoroughly. They should be blended well.

4. To this mixture, add the shredded chicken. Again mix thoroughly. You need to store this chicken salad for future use in an air-tight container.

5. If you want better results, you need to prepare the chicken salad a few hours before eating or serving it.

6. You can use this to serve with a sandwich or with bread lettuce. You can also serve it with any dish of your choice. If you want to bring in more variety, add a tablespoon or two tablespoons of green bell pepper. You can place this in any container that does not let air escape. You can store in air-tight containers for a maximum of four days.

7. If you want to make this recipe gluten-free, you need to check the ingredients' labels. Some store-bought chicken stock contains gluten. Avoid them if you are on a gluten-free diet.

Nutrition: Calories: 430 Carbs: 5g Protein: 41g Fat: 27g

Fiber: 1g

14.   Chipotle Grill Gluten-Free Steak

Preparation Time: 5 minutes

Cooking Time: 20 minutes

Servings: 4

Ingredients:

- 16 oz. skirt steak Black pepper & salt

- 1 homemade guacamole recipe

- 1 cup sour cream 1 handful fresh cilantro

- 4 oz. pepper jack cheese

- 1 splash Chipotle Tabasco Sauce

Directions:

1. Prepare the steak with a dusting of pepper and salt.

   Warm a cast-iron skillet using the high-temperature

   setting. Once hot, add the steak to cook for three to

four minutes per side. Let it rest on a plate while you

prepare the guacamole.

2. Prepare the guacamole according to the below

   recipe. Slice the steak against the grain into thin,

   bite-sized strips (4 portions).

3. Shred the pepper jack cheese using a cheese grater

   and sprinkle it over the steak.

4. Add about ¼ cup of guacamole to each portion,

   followed by ¼ cup of sour cream.

5. Splash each portion with sauce and fresh cilantro to

   serve.

Nutrition: Calories: 620 Protein: 33g

Net Carbs: 5.5g Fat: 50g

15. Chipotle Guacamole Sauce

Preparation Time: 5 minutes

Cooking Time: 10 minutes

Servings: 1

Ingredients:

- 2 ripe avocados

- 1 lime

- ¼ cup red onion

- 6 grape tomatoes

- 1 clove of garlic

- 1 tbsp. olive oil

- ⅛ tsp. black pepper

- ¼ tsp. salt

- Fresh cilantro

Optional: ⅛ tsp. crushed red pepper

Directions:

1. Do the prep. Juice the lime. Slice, remove the pit, and mash the avocados in a mixing container.

2. Dice the tomatoes and red onions. Add them to the avocado.

3. Mince the garlic clove and add the oil to combine.

4. Stir in the cilantro with the salt, pepper, crushed red pepper, and lime juice.

5. Thoroughly mix and serve with a steak bowl and a portion of pork rinds or low-carb crackers.

Nutrition: Calories: 155 Protein: 2g Carbs: 2g

Fat: 14g

16.   Chipotle Pork Carnitas

Preparation Time: 40 minutes

Cooking Time: 3 hours and 30 minutes

Servings: 12

Ingredients:

- 2 tbsp. of sunflower oil

- 4 lb. pork roast

- 1 tsp. salt

- 1 cup of water

- 1 tsp. thyme

- 2 tsp. - juniper berries

- ½ tsp. ground black pepper

Directions:

1. Set the temperature of your oven to 300 degrees Fahrenheit. This is to preheat the oven.

2. In the Dutch oven, add sunflower oil in medium flame. Use salt to season the roast. Once the oil is heated, sauté the roast on all sides. This will take three minutes per side.

3. You will brown the roast a bit when you sauté this way. You need to add bay leaves, juniper berries, water, thyme, and ground black pepper to the Dutch oven.

4. Close the pan with the lid. Cook this in the oven for three to four hours. In the pot, you need to keep turning the roast frequently. Only then, the flavors

will get into the roast, and it will incorporate the taste.

5. Take off the roast from the oven. Rest this for 20 minutes. Use two forks to pull the meat out of the pot.

6. Slow Cooker Directions: To a large skillet, add the sunflower oil. You can also add it to the Dutch oven and warm it using medium heat. When the oil gets hot, sauté the roast.

7. Place the meat into the slow cooker and add water, ground black pepper, thyme, bay leaves, and juniper berries.

8. Cover the cooker with a lid. Cook the meat for three to four hours using medium heat throughout the process. While cooking, turn the roast once in an

hour or once in 45 minutes or so. While you keep turning the roast less frequently, in this manner, you can ensure that the flavors get into the roast with ease.

9. If you want to use a pressure cooker for this recipe, it is not recommended. Only a slow cooker will ensure that the meat gets the perfect flavor. A fast cooking process using a pressure cooker will not give it a delicious flavor.

10. When you are choosing the pork, choose the cut that has marbling. Do not worry about the fat. You can always trim it.

11. If you do not prefer juniper berries, you can omit them. But the flavor would be altered when omitting juniper berries.

Note: For making the recipe keto-friendly, you can bring in avocado oil as a substitute to the sunflower oil.

Nutrition:

Calories: 223

Carbs: 0g

Protein: 33g

Fat: 8g

Fiber: 0g

Vegetables

17.   Mashed Cauliflower

Preparation Time: 20 Minutes

Cooking Time: 3 Hours **Servings:** 5

Ingredients:

- 3 tablespoons butter

- 1-pound cauliflower

- 1 tablespoon full-fat cream

- 1 teaspoon salt

- 1 teaspoon ground black pepper

- 1 oz dill, chopped

Directions:

1. Wash the cauliflower and chop it.

2. Place the chopped cauliflower in the slow cooker.

3. Add butter and full-fat cream.

4. Add salt and ground black pepper.

5. Stir the mixture and close the lid.

6. Cook the cauliflower for 3 hours on high.

7. When the cauliflower is cooked, transfer it to a blender and blend until smooth.

8. Place the smooth cauliflower in a bowl and mix it with the chopped dill.

9. Stir it well and serve!

Nutrition:

Calories 101 Fat 7.4g Fiber 3.2g Carbs 8.3g

Protein 3.1g

18.   Bacon-Wrapped Cauliflower

Preparation Time: 15 Minutes

Cooking Time: 7 Hours

Servings: 4

Ingredients:

- 11 oz cauliflower head

- 3 oz bacon, sliced

- 1 teaspoon salt

- 1 teaspoon cayenne pepper

- 1 oz butter, softened

- ¾ cup of water

Directions:

1. Sprinkle the cauliflower head with the salt and cayenne pepper then rub with butter.

2. Wrap the cauliflower head in the sliced bacon and secure with toothpicks.

3. Pour water in the slow cooker and add the wrapped cauliflower head.

4. Cook the cauliflower head for 7 hours on low.

5. Then let the cooked cauliflower head cool for 10 minutes.

6. Serve it!

Nutrition:

Calories 187

Fat 14.8g

Fiber 2.1g

Carbs 4.7g

Protein 9.5g

19.   Cauliflower Casserole

Preparation Time: 15 Minutes

Cooking Time: 7 Hours

Servings: 5

Ingredients:

- 2 tomatoes, chopped 11 oz cauliflower chopped

- 5 oz broccoli, chopped 1 cup of water

- 1 teaspoon salt

- 1 tablespoon butter

- 5 oz white mushrooms, chopped

- 1 teaspoon chili flakes

Directions:

1. Mix the water, salt, and chili flakes. Place the butter in
   the slow cooker.

2. Add a layer of the chopped cauliflower. Add the layer of broccoli and tomatoes.

3. Add the mushrooms and pat down the mix to flatten. Add the water and close the lid.

4. Cook the casserole for 7 hours on low. Cool the casserole to room temperature and serve!

Nutrition:

Calories 61

Fat 2.6g

Fiber 3.2g

Carbs 8.1g

Protein 3.4g

20.   Cauliflower Rice

Preparation Time: 15 Minutes

Cooking Time: 2 Hours

Servings: 5

Ingredients:

- 1-pound cauliflower

- 1 teaspoon salt

- 1 tablespoon turmeric

- 1 tablespoon butter

- ¾ cup of water

Directions:

1. Chop the cauliflower into tiny pieces to make cauliflower rice. You can also pulse in a food processor to get excellent grains of 'rice.'

2. Place the cauliflower rice in the slow cooker.

3. Add salt, turmeric, and water.

4. Stir gently and close the lid.

5. Cook the cauliflower rice for 2 hours on high.

6. Strain the cauliflower rice and transfer it to a bowl.

7. Add butter and stir gently. Serve it!

Nutrition:

Calories 48

Fat 2.5g

Fiber 2.6g

Carbs 5.7g

Protein 1.9g

21.   Curry Cauliflower

Preparation Time: 15 Minutes

Cooking Time: 5 Hours

Servings: 2

Ingredients:

- 10 oz cauliflower

- 1 teaspoon curry paste

- 1 teaspoon curry powder

- ½ teaspoon dried cilantro

- 1 oz butter ¾ cup of water

- ¼ cup chicken stock

Directions:

1. Chop the cauliflower roughly and sprinkle it with the curry powder and dried cilantro.

2. Place the chopped cauliflower in the slow cooker.

3. Mix the curry paste with the water.

4. Add chicken stock and transfer the liquid to the slow cooker.

5. Add butter and close the lid.

6. Cook the cauliflower for 5 hours on low.

7. Strain ½ of the liquid off and discard. Transfer the cauliflower to serving bowls. Serve it!

Nutrition:

Calories 158

Fat 13.3g

Fiber 3.9g

Carbs 8.9g

Protein 3.3g

22.   Garlic Cauliflower Steaks

Preparation Time: 15 Minutes

Cooking Time: 3 Hours

Servings: 4

Ingredients:

- 14 oz cauliflower head

- 1 teaspoon minced garlic

- 4 tablespoons butter

- 4 tablespoons water

- 1 teaspoon paprika

Directions:

1. Wash the cauliflower head carefully and slice it into the

   medium steaks.

2. Mix up together the butter, minced garlic, and paprika.

3. Rub the cauliflower steaks with the butter mixture.

4. Pour the water in the slow cooker.

5. Add the cauliflower steaks and close the lid.

6. Cook the vegetables for 3 hours on high.

7. Transfer the cooked cauliflower steaks to a platter and serve them immediately!

Nutrition:

Calories 129

Fat 11.7g

Fiber 2.7g

Carbs 5.8g

Protein 2.2g

Meat

23.   Ketogenic Meatballs

Preparation Time: 15 minutes

Cooking Time: 20 minutes

Servings: 10

Ingredients:

- 1 egg

- .5 cup Grated parmesan

- .5 cup Shredded mozzarella

- 1 lb. Ground beef

- 1 tbsp. garlic

Directions:

1. Warm-up the oven to reach 400. Combine all of the fixings.

2. Shape into meatballs. Bake within 18-20 minutes. Cool and serve.

Nutrition:

Net Carbohydrates: 0.7 grams

Protein: 12.2 grams

Total Fats: 10.9 grams

Calories: 153

24.   Roasted Leg of Lamb

Preparation Time: 15 minutes

Cooking Time: 1 hour & 30 minutes

Servings: 6

Ingredients:

- .5 cup Reduced-sodium beef broth

- 2 lb. lamb leg

- 6 garlic cloves

- 1 tbsp. rosemary leaves

- 1 tsp. Black pepper

Directions:

2. Warm-up oven temperature to 400 Fahrenheit.

3. Put the lamb in the pan and put the broth and seasonings.

4. Roast 30 minutes and lower the heat to 350° Fahrenheit. Cook within one hour.

5. Cool and serve.

Nutrition:

Net Carbohydrates: 1 gram

Protein: 22 grams

Total Fats: 14 grams

Calories: 223

Poultry and Eggs

25.   Chaffle with Scrambled Eggs

Preparation Time: 5 minutes

Cooking Time: 10 minutes;

Servings: 2

Ingredients

- 2 tsp coconut flour

- ½ cup shredded cheddar cheese, full-fat

- 3 eggs

- 1-ounce butter, unsalted

- Seasoning:

- ¼ tsp salt

- 1/8 tsp ground black pepper

- 1/8 tsp dried oregano

Directions:

1. Switch on a mini waffle maker and let it preheat for 5 minutes.

2. Meanwhile, take a medium bowl, place all the ingredients in it, reserving 2 eggs and then mix by using an immersion blender until smooth.

3. Ladle the batter evenly into the waffle maker, shut with lid, and let it cook for 3 to 4 minutes until firm and golden brown.

4. Meanwhile, prepare scrambled eggs and for this, take a medium bowl, crack the eggs in it and whisk them with a fork until frothy, and then season with salt and black pepper.

5. Take a medium skillet pan, place it over medium heat, add butter and when it melts, pour in eggs and cook for 2 minutes until creamy, stirring continuously.

6. Top chaffles with scrambled eggs, sprinkle with oregano, and then serve.

Nutrition: 265 Calories; 18.5 g Fats; 17.6 g Protein; 3.4 g Net Carb; 6 g Fiber;

26. Sheet Pan Eggs with Mushrooms and Spinach

Preparation Time: 5 minutes

Cooking Time: 12 minutes;

Servings: 2

Ingredients

- 2 eggs

- 1 tsp chopped jalapeno pepper

- 1 tbsp. chopped mushrooms

- 1 tbsp. chopped spinach

- 1 tbsp. chopped chard

- Seasoning:

- 1/3 tsp salt

- 1/4 tsp ground black pepper

Directions:

1. Turn on the oven, then set it to 350 degrees F and let it preheat.

2. Take a medium bowl, crack eggs in it, add salt and black pepper, then add all the vegetables and stir until combined.

3. Take a medium sheet ball or rimmed baking sheet, grease it with oil, pour prepared egg batter on it, and then bake for 10 to 12 minutes until done.

4. Cut egg into two squares and then serve.

Nutrition: 165 Calories; 10.7 g Fats; 14 g Protein; 1.5 g Net Carb; 0.5 g Fiber;

Seafood

27.   Tuna with Vegetables

Preparation Time: 5 minutes;

Cooking Time: 15 minutes

Servings: 2

Ingredients

- 4 oz. tuna, packed in water

- 2 oz. broccoli florets

- ½ of red bell pepper, cored, sliced

- ½ tsp minced garlic

- ½ tsp sesame seeds

- Seasoning:

- 1 tbsp. avocado oil

- 2/3 tsp soy sauce

- 2/3 tsp apple cider vinegar

- 3 tbsp. water

Directions:

1. Take a skillet pan, add ½ tbsp. oil and when hot, add bell pepper and cook for 3 minutes until tender-crisp.

2. Then add broccoli floret, drizzle with water and continue cooking for 3 minutes until steamed, covering the pan.

3. Uncover the pan, cook for 2 minutes until all the liquid has evaporated, and then push bell pepper to one side of the pan.

4. Add remaining oil to the other side of the pan, add tuna and cook for 3 minutes until seared on all sides.

5. Then drizzle with soy sauce and vinegar, toss all the ingredients in the pan until mixed and sprinkle with sesame seeds.

6. Serve.

Nutrition: 99.7 Calories; 5.1 g Fats; 11 g Protein; 1.6 g Net Carb; 1 g Fiber

28.   Chili-glazed Salmon

Preparation Time: 5 minutes

Cooking Time: 10 minutes

Servings: 2

Ingredients

- 2 salmon fillets

- 2 tbsp. sweet chili sauce

- 2 tsp chopped chives

- ½ tsp sesame seeds

Directions:

1. Turn on the oven, then set it to 400 degrees F and let it preheat.

2. Meanwhile, place salmon in a shallow dish, add chili sauce and chives and toss until mixed.

3. Transfer prepared salmon onto a baking sheet lined with parchment sheet, drizzle with remaining sauce and bake for 10 minutes until thoroughly cooked.

4. Garnish with sesame seeds and Serve.

Nutrition: 112.5 Calories; 5.6 g Fats; 12 g Protein; 3.4 g Net Carb; 0 g Fiber

29.   Baked Tilapia

Preparation Time: 20 minutes

Cooking Time: 40 minutes

Servings: 4

Ingredients:

- 4 tilapia fillets

- 1 lemon zest

- 2 tablespoons fresh lemon juice

- 1 tablespoon garlic, minced

- ¼ cup butter, melted

- 2 tablespoons fresh parsley, chopped

- Pepper Salt

Directions:

1. Preheat the oven to 4250 F.

2. In a small bowl, mix together butter, lemon zest, lemon juice, and garlic and set aside.

3. Season fish fillets with pepper and salt.

4. Place fish fillets onto the baking dish. Pour butter mixture over fish fillets.

5. Bake fish in a preheated oven for 10-12 minutes.

6. Garnish with parsley and serve.

Nutrition:

Calories: 247

Fat: 13.6 grams

Net Carbs: 1 gram

Protein: 32.4 grams

30.   emony Sea Bass Fillet

Preparation Time: 10 minutes

Cooking Time: 10-15 minutes

Servings: 4

Ingredients:

Fish:

4 sea bass fillets

2 tablespoons olive oil, divided

A pinch of chili pepper

Salt, to taste

Olive Sauce:

1 tablespoon green olives, pitted and sliced

1 lemon, juiced

Salt, to taste

Directions:

Preheat the grill to high heat.

Stir together one tablespoon olive oil, chili pepper, and salt in a bowl.

Brush both sides of each sea bass fillet generously with the mixture.

Grill the fillets on the preheated grill for about 5 to 6 minutes on each side until lightly browned.

Meanwhile, warm the left olive oil in a skillet over medium heat.

Add the green olives, lemon juice, and salt.

Cook until the sauce is heated through.

Transfer the fillets to four serving plates, then pour the sauce over them. Serve warm.

Nutrition:

Calories: 257

Fat: 12.4g

Fiber: 56.g

Carbohydrates:2 g

Protein: 12.7g

31.   Curried Fish

Preparation Time: 10 minutes

Cooking Time: 20 minutes

Servings: 4

Ingredients:

2 tablespoons coconut oil 2 teaspoons garlic, minced

11/2 tablespoons grated fresh ginger

1/2 teaspoon ground cumin 1 tablespoon curry powder

2 cups of coconut milk

16 ounces (454 g) firm white fish, cut into 1-inch chunks

1 cup kale, shredded 2 tablespoons cilantro, chopped

Directions:

Melt the coconut oil in a heated pan

Add the garlic and ginger and sauté for about 2 minutes until tender.

Fold in the cumin and curry powder, then cook for 1 to 2 minutes until fragrant.

Put in the coconut milk and boil. Boil then simmer until the flavors mellow, about 5 minutes.

Add the fish chunks and simmer for 10 minutes until the fish flakes easily with a fork, stirring once.

Scatter the shredded kale and chopped cilantro over the fish, then cook for 2 minutes more until softened.

Nutrition:

Calories: 376 Fat: 19.9g

Fiber: 15.8g Carbohydrates: 6.7 g

Protein: 14.8 g

32.   Shrimp Alfredo

Preparation Time: 15 minutes

Cooking Time: 30 minutes

Servings: 4

Ingredients:

1 pound of wild shrimp

3 tablespoons of organic grass-fed whey

1 1/2 cups of frozen asparagus

1 cup of heavy cream

1/2 cup of parmesan cheese

Sea salt

Black pepper

2 ground garlic cloves

1 small diced onion

Directions:

Peel and devein the shrimps, coat them well with salt and pepper. Let it cover in a bowl for 20 minutes.

Preheat a skillet. Put in butter, garlic, and onions.

When butter is melted, put in shrimp and stir fry till for 3 minutes.

Pour in heavy cream and stir well. Then, add ion cheese and stir till cheese melts.

Serve hot.

Nutrition:

Calories: 315 Fat: 11.9g Fiber: 8.5g Carbohydrates:9.3 g

Protein: 11.1g

33.   Keto Fish & Chips

Preparation Time: 15 minutes

Cooking Time: 30 minutes

Servings: 2

Ingredients:

For chips:

½ tbsp olive oil

1 medium zucchini

Salt

pepper

For fish:

¾ lb. cod

Oil

½ cup almond flour

¼ tsp onion powder

For Sauce:

2 tbsp dill pickle relish

¼ tbsp curry powder

½ cup mayonnaise

½ tsp paprika powder

½ cup parmesan cheese

1 egg

Salt

pepper

Directions:

Mix all the sauce fixing in a bowl. Set aside.

Warm-up oven to 400°F. Make thin zucchini rods, brush with oil, and spread on the baking sheet. Put salt and pepper then bake within 30 minutes.

Beat the egg in a bowl. On a separate plate, combine the parmesan cheese, almond flour, and the remaining spices.

Slice the fish into 1 inch by 1-inch pieces. Roll them on the flour mixture. Dip in the beaten egg and then in the flour again. Fry the fish for three minutes. Serve.

Nutrition:

Calories 463

Fat 26.2 g

Protein 49g

Carbs 6g

Snacks

34.   Cauliflower Tartar Bread

Preparation Time: 10 minutes

Cooking Time: 50 minutes

Servings: 4

Ingredients:

- 3 cup cauliflower rice

- 10 large eggs, yolks and egg whites separated

- ¼ tsp cream of tartar

- 1 ¼ cup coconut flour

- 1 ½ tbsp. gluten-free baking powder

- 1 tsp sea salt

- 6 tbsp. butter

- 6 cloves garlic, minced

- 1 tbsp. fresh rosemary, chopped

- 1 tbsp. fresh parsley, chopped

Directions:

1. Preheat your oven to 350 degrees F. Layer a 9x5-inch pan with wax paper.

2. Place the cauliflower rice in a suitable bowl and then cover it with plastic wrap.

3. Heat it for 4 minutes in the microwave. Heat more if the cauliflower isn't soft enough.

4. Place the cauliflower rice in a kitchen towel and squeeze it to drain excess water.

5. Transfer drained cauliflower rice to a food processor.

6. Add coconut flour, sea salt, baking powder, butter, egg yolks, and garlic. Blend until crumbly.

7. Beat egg whites with cream of tartar in a bowl until foamy.

8. Add egg white mixture to the cauliflower mixture and stir well with a spatula.

9. Fold in rosemary and parsley.

10. Spread this batter in the prepared baking pan evenly.

11. Bake it for 50 minutes until golden then allow it to cool.

Nutrition:

Calories: 104

Fat: 8.9 g

Cholesterol: 57 mg

Sodium: 340 mg

Carbohydrates: 4.7 g

35.   **Wrapped Bacon Cheeseburger**

Preparation Time: 23 minutes

Cooking Time: 20 minutes

Servings: 4

Ingredients:

- 7 oz. bacon

- 1 ½ pounds ground beef

- ½ teaspoon salt

- ¼ teaspoon pepper

- 4 oz. cheese, shredded

- 1 head iceberg or romaine lettuce, leaves parted and

  washed

- 1 tomato, sliced

- ¼ pickled cucumber, finely sliced

Directions:

1. Cook bacon and set aside.

2. In a separate bowl, combine ground beef, salt, and pepper. Divide mixture into 4 sections, create balls and press each one slightly to form a patty.

3. Put your patties into a frying pan and cook for about 4 minutes on each side.

4. Top each cooked patty with a slice of cheese, several pieces of bacon, and pickled cucumber. Add a bit of tomato.

5. Wrap each burger in a big lettuce leaf.

Nutrition:

Calories: 684 Fat: 51 grams

Net Carbs: 5 grams Protein: 48 grams

36.   Crab Dip

Preparation Time: 15 minutes

Cooking Time: 0 minutes **Servings:** 12

Ingredients:

Lemon juice, 1tsp Chives, 2tbsp

1/2tsp Old Bay seasoning Sour cream, 3tbsp

8oz Crabmeat 4oz Cream cheese

Directions:

Mix the cream cheese, lemon juice, seasoning, and sour cream.

Fold the crab meat, then the chives, stirring. Serve.

Nutrition:

Calories 42 Fat 4g Protein 5g

Carbs 3g

Salads

37.   Cucumber Salad

Preparation Time: 10 Minutes

Cooking Time: 0

Servings: 4

Ingredients:

1/3 cup cucumber basil ranch

1 cucumber, chopped

3 tomatoes, chopped

3 tbsp fresh herbs, chopped

½ onion, sliced

Directions:

Add all ingredients into the large mixing bowl and toss well.

Serve immediately and enjoy.

Nutrition:

Calories 84

Fat 3.4 g

Carbs 12.5 g

Protein 2 g

Soups and Stews

38.   Tomato Basil Soup

Preparation Time: 10 minutes

Cooking Time: 40 minutes

Servings: 4

Ingredients:

¼ cup olive oil

½ cup heavy cream

1 lb. tomatoes, fresh

4 cup chicken broth, divided

4 cloves garlic, fresh

Sea salt & pepper to taste

Directions:

Preheat oven to 400° Fahrenheit and line a baking sheet with foil.

Remove the cores from your tomatoes and place them on the baking sheet along with the cloves of garlic.

Drizzle tomatoes and garlic with olive oil, salt, and pepper.

Roast at 400° Fahrenheit for 30 minutes.

Pull the tomatoes out of the oven and place into a blender, along with the juices that have dripped onto the pan during roasting.

Add two cups of the chicken broth to the blender.

Blend until smooth, then strain the mixture into a large saucepan or a pot.

While the pan is on the stove, whisk the remaining two cups of broth and the cream into the soup.

Simmer for about ten minutes.

Season to taste, then serve hot!

Nutrition:

Calories: 225

Carbohydrates: 5.5 g

Fat: 20 g

Protein: 6.5 g

39.   Chicken Enchilada Soup

Preparation Time: 10 minutes

Cooking Time: 45 minutes

Servings: 4

Ingredients:

½ cup fresh cilantro, chopped

1 ¼ tsp. chili powder

1 cup fresh tomatoes, diced

1 med. yellow onion, diced

1 small red bell pepper, diced

1 tbsp. cumin, ground

1 tbsp. extra virgin olive oil

1 tbsp. lime juice, fresh

1 tsp. dried oregano

2 cloves garlic, minced

2 lg. stalks celery, diced

4 cups chicken broth

8 oz. chicken thighs, boneless & skinless, shredded

8 oz. cream cheese, softened

Directions:

In a pot over medium heat, warm olive oil.

Once hot, add celery, red pepper, onion, and garlic. Cook for about 3 minutes or until shiny.

Stir the tomatoes into the pot and let cook for another 2 minutes.

Add seasonings to the pot, stir in chicken broth and bring to a boil.

Once boiling, drop the heat down to low and allow to simmer for 20 minutes.

Once simmered, add the cream cheese and allow the soup to return to a boil. *

Drop the heat once again and allow to simmer for another 20 minutes.

Stir the shredded chicken into the soup along with the lime juice and the cilantro.

Spoon into bowls and serve hot!

Nutrition:

Calories: 420 Carbohydrates: 9 g

Fat: 29.5 g Protein: 27 g

DESSERTS

40.   Cheesecake with a Biscuit Base

Preparation: 40 min

Ready in 1 h 20 min

Ingredients

- 150 g whole grain biscuit

- 50 g butter

- 1 tbsp beet syrup

- 500 g ricotta

- 300 g low-fat quark

- 2 eggs

- 2 tbsp food starch

- ½ tsp vanilla powder

- 50 g raw cane sugar

- 100 g chopped almond

- 150 g small candy bars

- 150 ml whipped cream

Preparation steps

1. In a clean tea towel, place the biscuits and use the rolling pine for crumbling. Melt the butter and sugar beet syrup in a small casserole over low heats and mix. Line the

bakery paper in the spring shape pot. Pour the mixture into the biscuit and squeeze it down.

2. Mix the quark with the ricotta. Add egg, whisk, vanilla powder, and sugar to the macerated starch gradually. Fold in the cream of the almonds. Put the chocolate bars on the bottom of the cake and smooth over it. In a pre-heated oven, cook for 50-60 minutes at 180 ° C (convection 160 ° C; gas: 2-3)

3. Taken out of the oven, let the cheesecake cool in the pot for a while. Remove from the mould the cheesecake and leave to cool completely.

4. Shake the cream into the steepness and serve the cake.

CPSIA information can be obtained
at www.ICGtesting.com
Printed in the USA
BVHW082032100521
606946BV00006B/1255

9 781801 411882